I0481548

NetWorth
Lending

NetWorth Lending

NETWORTH LENDING

For permission requests or general information contact:
www.iamtammylewis.com

DISCLAIMER: This book is intended for informational purposes only.

Published and Edited by IDEAL Book Publishing

NetWorth Lending

ISBN   978-1983575150

CONTENTS

HOW TO USE THIS BOOK

Books are used for all sorts of things, from coffee coasters to decoration. Like you, I'm of the belief that we learn best from books we actually read. This book was designed to be read in one sitting, to make sure your time investment is well rewarded.

There are two distinct but interconnected sections in this book. The first is a compilation of mortgage tips and advice to help you better understand the mortgage process and avoid common pitfalls. The second delves into the *NetWorth Lending* philosophy and process. You will benefit most by reading each chapter in order, since each section builds on the next and is essential to understanding the full concept.

INTRODUCTION

The year was 1935 and America was in the throes of the
Great Depression. The dream that once fueled the
hopes of a nation had degenerated into a paralyzing
nightmare. Visions of a better life and opportunity
were dashed to a thousand pieces and like humpty
dumpty, broken beyond repair. From this calamitous
period the seeds of most of our current mortgage
philosophies were fertilized and grew into the
immovable redwoods of industry norms we have come
to accept as law.

We have driverless cars, phones small enough to fit in
our pockets with computing power and versatility that
was once inconceivable. The explosion of knowledge
about our world and our place in it, is unprecedented in
human history, yet many approach the mortgage
process the same way our great grandparents did
without ever questioning why. This book is intended to
put context around the status quo and beckon you to
dig deeper into this topic of immense importance. Before
we journey too far, I must readily concede that some of

the concepts in this book are not new. They are proven and essential to the financially literate.

NetWorth Lending is my personal mortgage philosophy. It teaches people how to use their mortgage as an unparalleled tool to get out of debt sooner and retire with more money. It is not intended to be a one size fits all solution. The ultimate value of any mortgage solution should be weighed on the merits of how it fits and improves *your* individual situation. If it's appropriate, the numbers will support it and you can move forward confidently knowing you've made an informed decision. It is my sincere hope and desire that this book will cause people to identify and evaluate their current mortgage philosophy and compare it with *NetWorth Lending*. If each reader understands the concepts in this book and takes this vital step, I will consider my efforts a resounding success. I am beyond excited to share these concepts with you because of the tremendous impact they can have in your family's quest for financial independence.

CHAPTER 1

CADS
THE KEY TO MORTGAGE QUALIFYING

CREDIT

WHEN IT COMES TO IDENTIFYING mortgage qualifying criteria, there are competing opinions that make it challenging to determine what really matters. While many factors have a bearing on both the interest rate and programs you may qualify for, four factors impact the outcome more than the rest. They are: Credit, Affordability, Down-Payment, and Stability (CADS). Similar to a car that needs four properly inflated tires to function, each portion of CADS is critical to the qualification process. If one or more is deficient, you may not be able to obtain a mortgage.

The credit factor consists of two distinct parts: the score and accounts. A mortgage credit score is the middle of three scores, or the lower middle score if there are two borrowers. Scores are broken into various tiers and can exceed 800 points. Scores above 780 represent the highest qualifying level, and every twenty points less represent the next tier (i.e. 759-740, 739-720, etc.)

A credit score is a numerical representation of risk. It's a forecast to the lender of the likelihood of the borrower becoming ninety days or more delinquent on an account within the next two years.[1] In short, the higher the score, the less risk to the creditor and vice versa. If your credit score is below 780, you may have to pay a little more to obtain credit.[2]

For Account Development, it's ideal to have at least three tradelines open, for a minimum of 24 months, one with a high credit limit of $5000.00 or more. There shouldn't be any collections, judgments, late payments or derogatory marks within the previous two years. (Bankruptcy or Foreclosure's may require additional time to be acceptable.)

To preserve or raise your credit scores aim to keep credit card balances below 30% of their limit; minimize credit inquiries; avoid accounts from finance companies or other higher-risk creditors; and make payments on or before their due date. Credit card accounts above 30% of their limit, and accounts from finance companies, will not give you the maximum possible score even when payments are made on time. Credit inquiries can also reduce your scores.

You should be very selective and allow access on an as-needed basis only.

AFFORDABILITY

When investing, wisdom says you should not be concerned with the return "on" an investment more than the return "of" your investment. This statement succinctly captures the "why" behind affordability in mortgage qualifying.

It's important to understand mortgage lenders are in the investing business; their investment just happens to be secured by real estate. The primary way a mortgage lender makes money is from on-time payments until the debt is repaid. When a mortgage goes into default, everyone loses. Foreclosure is expensive and can cost tens of thousands of dollars. With all of this at risk, it's easy to see how vital it is to make a sound lending decision for both the borrower and lender.

Affordability, or the debt-to-income ratio, is expressed as a front side and backside percentage. The front side ratio is a comparison of your gross monthly income to the proposed house payment. The house payment consists of principal and interest (P&I), property taxes (T), homeowner and mortgage insurances (I) and homeowner's association dues (A) (PITIA).

The backside ratio is calculated by adding the sum of other monthly recurring expenses to the proposed mortgage payment and dividing that by your gross monthly income. Other recurring expenses include payments for autos, credit cards, installment loans, other mortgages, child support, etc. Generally, any debt with more than ten remaining payments should be included in the total. (Excluding utilities and living expenses like groceries.)

Baseline front and backside ratios for conventional loans are 28% and 36% respectively. These percentages can vary depending on the loan type and program. Typically, a backside ratio less than 43% is considered prudent. (Incidentally, this is one of the requirements for a loan to be considered a *qualified mortgage*. A mortgage with this designation can offer additional protection to both the borrower and lender.)

A quick way to estimate affordability is to use $400.00 for every $1000.00 of your gross income and subtract your other monthly expenses. The difference would be the estimated mortgage payment you can afford.

Let's say you earn $5000.00 a month and your other monthly expenses total $750.00. When we set aside $400.00 of every $1000.00 in income you have a total of $2000.00 of affordability. ($400.00 x 5= $2000.00)

Subtract your other expenses from this number and you will know the approximate mortgage payment you can afford.

($2000.00 - $750.00 = $1250.00 Mortgage Payment)

It's important to determine what you qualify for and how much your family can afford to spend upfront. Sometimes there is a difference between the two figures. Will going to the top of your qualifying range still allow you to save money for unexpected events, retirement goals, vacations, etc.? Will you be able to pay your bills on or before their due date? If you aren't certain, reduce the amount you allocate for the mortgage payment. The surest way to enjoy your home is by purchasing one that works well with your overall goals.

<u>DOWN PAYMENT</u>

A down payment reflects a borrower's willingness to share risk with the lender. Mandating a large down payment was once considered the only prudent approach to lending. In fact, after a housing bust in the 1800's, federally chartered banks were prevented from loaning more than 50% of a property's value. Only a few could afford homes, and most people became perpetual renters.

Residential mortgages in the early 1900's were quite different than today's options. Terms were typically one to five years with interest only amortization and a balloon payment. Borrowers had to make a down payment of half of the home's value and either refinance the mortgage or pay it off completely at the end of the mortgage term.

After the Great Depression and the implementation of several lending laws, extended mortgage terms with smaller down payments became commonplace. The Federal Housing Administration (FHA) provided loss protection to lenders in case of foreclosure and they introduced term lengths of up to twenty years with fully amortizing payments. Down payments shrunk to as little as 10% with FHA insured loans and made the dream of homeownership a reality for many families.

Decades later, the birth of Fannie Mae, Freddie Mac, and the private mortgage insurance industry were essential in moving the homeownership needle forward in the United States. Mortgage Guaranty Insurance Corporation (MGIC) was the first private mortgage insurer in the country. They were able to provide loss protection to lenders faster than FHA and at better rates for consumers. Unlike FHA however, they only protected a percentage of the mortgage for a fixed period. (Typically, until the equity position reached 20%.) This model made sense but was only available for the most qualified buyers.

Borrowers that qualified for private mortgage insurance were typically less risky than FHA clients and in time, down payments shrunk to as little as 5% of the purchase price.

This privatization led to another explosion in mortgage lending and made larger homes affordable. This seismic shift is most evident in the multiplication of our home's square footage. In the early 1900's, 800 square feet was the average home size. Today, it's well over 2200 square feet!

Smaller down payments have unquestionably led to an increase in homeownership but represent a decrease in risk sharing by borrowers. Even with mortgage insurance protection, lenders expect an increase in the rate of return, or interest rate of the loan to embrace this risk.

STABILITY

Can you predict the future? Each day people follow all sorts of rituals trying to glimpse what's to come. How would you like to be responsible for predicting the future, and make decisions worth hundreds of thousands of dollars based on that insight? How would you do it? Could you do it? That's close to what a lender does every time a loan is made that will be repaid over two or more decades. They are betting on how the future of that investment will look.

While it's nearly impossible to forecast the success or failure of our favorite sports team, generally people are predictable. We are creatures of habit and tend to do what we've always done. While that may be disastrous for dieting, it's helpful when making an educated guess of how a person may repay a mortgage.

Lenders evaluate the last two years of employment, residential and credit histories, and saving patterns to determine a borrower's stability. This time frame gives a wide enough view of how they've handled financial responsibilities and is the universally accepted time frame for stability consideration. When you apply for a mortgage, be prepared with addresses for all the places you've worked and lived and explanations for any derogatory credit marks within this time frame.

While a two-year time frame is a good indicator of how we are likely to handle things in the future, what happened in the most recent twelve months is critical. How many jobs have you had? Has your income trended up or down? Are there late payments or other derogatory marks? If so, what caused them, and why won't it affect a potential mortgage payment from being impacted in the future? Understand the story your stability relays and be prepared to address anything that is less than favorable or unusual.

Documenting a habit of savings is also very important. Lenders review the most recent sixty days of retirement and checking and savings accounts to document stability. If there are large deposits or unusual transactions, additional documentation and explanations will be required.

References:

1. *https://www.consumer.ftc.gov/articles/0152-credit-scores*
2. *http://files.consumerfinance.gov/f/201503_cfpb_your-home-loan-toolkit-web.pdf*

CHAPTER 2

COMPONENTS OF A HOUSE PAYMENT

THERE ARE FOUR COMPONENTS TO a house payment: Principal and Interest, Taxes, Insurance(s) and Association dues. (PITIA) All four categories should be considered to get an accurate picture of your home's true monthly cost.

Principal and Interest (P&I) are components of the mortgage. Each month as the mortgage amortizes, the principal portion of the payment reduces the principal balance and the rest is applied to interest. Interest is the amount a lender charges for using their funds. Initially, the lion's share of the mortgage payment is applied towards interest. As time progresses the pendulum gradually swings the other way and more of the payment is applied to the principal balance than interest. Loans with an interest only repayment option are just paying the cost of borrowing the money each month and not reducing the principal at all. While there are certain situations where this type of repayment may make sense, most loans are fully amortizing, and a portion of the monthly payment is applied to principal and interest.

The "T" represents real estate taxes. Depending on where in the country your home is located, you may have several taxes associated with real estate ownership. The frequency, type, calculation method, and amount can vary drastically. For example, in my area of the country, there are city and county taxes that must be paid annually. In other municipalities, additional assessments are not uncommon, and payments may be due as frequently as once a quarter.

The "I" stands for insurances. If you haven't made at least a twenty percent down payment, and I don't necessarily think that you always should, you will likely have mortgage insurance. Mortgage insurance gives the lender some financial protection in case of foreclosure, in exchange for providing a mortgage with a reduced down payment. Homeowners or hazard insurance, as it is often referred to, protects you and the lender from fire, accidents, theft and damage to the house. While there are instances where mortgage insurance may not be required, homeowner's insurance must remain in place if you have a mortgage. When your mortgage is paid off, this type of insurance is no longer mandated, but the risk of not maintaining it is unnecessarily high.

The last portion of the house payment is homeowner's association dues "A". A homeowner's association is a group organized for planned unit developments, condos and subdivisions to protect, preserve and enhance properties. They typically maintain landscaping in common areas, create and enforce community design and appearance rules, hold meetings, and have the authority to assess fines. When run effectively, homeowner's associations can be a valuable means to preserve a community. Although rare, they also can foreclose on properties if their dues are not paid.

CHAPTER 3

MORTGAGE ORIGINATORS

WHEN IT COMES TO MORTGAGE ORIGINATORS, there are three main players; Mortgage Brokers, Banks & Credit Unions, and Mortgage Banks. Each one can offer mortgages, but there are important differences which can impact the way a loan is obtained. To understand the differences between these entities, we'll describe the common steps in a mortgage process and show how each one varies.

The first step in the mortgage process is for a client to make an application. Their credit report is obtained, coupled with the information from the application and compared to various program guidelines. This process is prequalification.

Afterwards the originator requests documents to validate the data from the application. The documentation is reviewed, and an automated underwriting decision is issued to determine if the borrower should qualify for a loan program. This is considered a preapproval.

The client determines if the loan meets their needs and signs preliminary documents to begin the process.

After this, the appraisal, title search and other verifications such as employment, deposit, rental payments, etc., are ordered. The application and all other documentation, must be reviewed by an underwriter to determine if the borrower's scenario meets the selected program's guidelines. If it does, but there are additional questions, the underwriter requests loan conditions that must be provided before the loan is approved. This is referred to as a Conditional Approval.

The loan conditions are requested from the client. Once obtained, the file is sent back to the underwriter for review. If all items are acceptable, a final approval is issued. However, if the underwriter still has questions or determines the items do not satisfy the program requirements, more conditions are issued. This process repeats until all conditions are satisfied or it's determined the loan cannot be approved

Once final approval is issued to the originator, the loan is scheduled for closing. The closing department corresponds with the client's attorney or title company to prepare documents for the borrower to sign. They provide a list of items to the closing attorney/title company that must be completed before they will release the loan funds.

Once a borrower signs the closing paperwork and all the funding requirements are met, the loan is funded, meaning the actual money is sent. Although this is an oversimplification of the overall process, it gives us a framework to understand the differences between originators.

A mortgage broker typically works with several different banks to provide a variety of loan products for their customers. They don't have money to fund any loans they originate. Brokers are at the mercy of the banks they work for to determine the suitability of a borrower's scenario which means they have low control. A borrower's loan package must be submitted to the bank's underwriter for review. These banks usually provide mortgages directly to consumers as well as offering their products to mortgage brokers. When this is the case, broker submissions will not take priority over the bank's originations. This means there may be delays in the process when dealing with a broker. Additionally, since the underwriter and closing department work for the bank, brokers have less influence to get exceptions or rushes for a transaction. If a bank's guidelines change, the broker may not get updated immediately and can submit a loan scenario that was once acceptable but no longer is.

Banks and Credit Unions provide many other services in addition to mortgages. Their lending products are only *one way* to serve their customers. While it's important to them, it's not their primary focus. They tend to be very selective with the kind of client they originate for since they want to be able to offer them other products. Contrary to popular belief, banks don't always have the most competitive rates and their program selection is usually limited to fit a specific client type. The time it takes to close a loan with them can be extended because they only allot so much manpower and resources to the mortgage process. When they are overwhelmed, they tend to be very slow to hire and choose to increase the time it takes to close a loan rather than increase fixed costs for additional manpower.

The last originator type is a mortgage banker. As the name suggests, it's a hybrid of the other two originators. With this originator you get the best of both worlds. They have high control since they lend their own money and have a strong structure. They have their own underwriters and closing department like a bank, but unlike a bank they only offer mortgages. Since this is all they do, their entire business is focused on providing mortgages. Like a mortgage broker, they have a wide variety of programs and products to offer. This allows them to help a broader range of clients than a bank with more speed and control than a broker.

Service is usually highest with this originator and closings happen more quickly. This type of originator tends to attract more experienced loan professionals from banks and mortgage brokers for these reasons.

Regardless of the originator type, the loan officer you choose is equally important. A poor choice in loan officer will exaggerate the weaknesses of any originator type.

CHAPTER 4

HOW TO AVOID THE 5 MOST COMMON MISTAKES AFTER APPLYING FOR A MORTGAGE

THERE IS A MOUNTAIN OF information available at the click of a mouse discussing what you should do to get ready to apply for a mortgage. Although it's not discussed nearly as often, what you do after you have made an application is vitally important. I'll highlight five items that will preserve your qualifying power and reduce the chances of catastrophe.

1) **Don't let anyone else pull your credit**. When I say anyone, I mean anyone, once you've applied for a loan. I could write that two more times to underscore its importance if it weren't redundant. The best time to compare lenders is before you have your credit pulled, not after. Once your credit is pulled, it's necessary for you to preserve your scores. Additional inquiries can have a negative impact on your scores, and there is no scenario where lowering your scores is good for you.

2) **Don't open new accounts**. I know it will be tempting to buy that perfect set of furniture for your living room or that new car, but please don't. New accounts mean new payments and a reduction in your qualifying power. You are making the largest investment you will likely ever make when you get a mortgage. Isn't it best to prioritize and protect it? Is taking advantage of that sale worth your new home? Do you like that new car enough to live in it? OK am I going overboard? Slightly. Is it warranted? Absolutely! The time to get those things you've always wanted is after your loan funds and you get the keys to your new home. Until then don't open or add any new accounts or debts.

3) **Continue making <u>all</u> payments on time.** You've probably heard mortgage-related credit reports are good for 90 days and that is typically true. It's easy to get caught up in the whirlwind of moving and forget things you normally wouldn't. Please take extra care to ensure all your payments are made on, or before time. It's not uncommon for individual accounts to be refreshed before closing or your credit report may have to be re-pulled depending on its expiration date. One late payment, no matter how small the account, can change your scores in a major way.

Don't change jobs or employment type. Once you've applied for a loan, please don't make changes to your income. This is not the time to transition from W2 income to self-employment or decide that you've had enough and quit to find a better opportunity. Any change to your income profile causes the mortgage process to screech to a neck-snapping halt. If you think you are going to have a change in income soon, it's far better to delay applying for a mortgage until after that change is completed and documented. To use income from a new job, you may need to show receipt of pay stubs in addition to an offer letter. (Self-employment income requires a track record of 2 years.) A 30-day delay can be significant if your closing is in 2 weeks and the movers are already scheduled. Think twice and plan accordingly to avoid an unnecessary delay and disappointment.

4) **Build in a time buffer**. In today's market it's not uncommon for a borrower to sell their existing home in the morning and close on their new home in the afternoon with the proceeds of that sale. While this can happen, the likelihood of things going wrong is immense. What if the buyers for your existing property have a delay and can't close on time?

There are many reasons why this could happen, almost none of which you can control. Are you living out of boxes in preparation for the closing? Are your belongings already on the moving truck? If they are, you could be playing a dangerous game. It's far better to schedule the closings at least a week apart. This applies to renters moving to a new home as well. Plan to have a place to stay for at least a week after you close to allot for any unforeseen hiccups. Will it require more planning and cost a little extra? Yes. The peace of mind your family will have through the process by taking this one simple step however, will be well worth the cost.

CHAPTER 5

WHY DIDN'T I GET
THE RATE I SAW ON THE INTERNET?

WE GET BOMBARDED WITH THOUSANDS of advertising messages each day. Companies know to get your attention they must have a very attractive hook to get you to pay attention. Most mortgage companies use a low interest rate advertisement to get the job done. If you look closely at the fine print however, you'll discover the advertised rate applies to very limited scenarios.

There also are some valid reasons why the interest rate you ultimately get may be different than what was advertised. Let's explore the most common reasons.

1) **They haven't pulled your credit or reviewed your documentation.** Earlier, we provided an overview of the mortgage process and called out the difference between a prequalification and preapproval. A prequalification is nothing more than an educated guess.

Many times, an application can appear to meet loan requirements until there has been a thorough review of the supporting documentation. Mortgage programs can be quite complex and nuanced. For example, the handbook for FHA mortgages is over one thousand pages and that is only for one type of loan! Programs may have pages of guidelines. Omitting or failing to meet one of them can mean not being able to qualify at all.

2) **Loan Level Price Adjustments.** Loan level price adjustments are fees charged to lenders that sell mortgages to Fannie Mae and Freddie Mac as an offset for accepting mortgages with certain risk factors. The loan size, purpose, occupancy type and credit score are just a few of the things that are considered. Lenders will typically pass these costs onto the borrower in the form of a higher interest rate. These adjustments do not apply to FHA, VA and USDA loans. For more information see these links:

https://www.fanniemae.com/content/pricing/llpa-matrix.pdf

http://www.freddiemac.com/singlefamily/pdf/ex19.pdf

3) **Your rate is not locked.** Mortgage rates can move up and down several times a day, let alone in a week. When a rate is locked, it protects you from an increase in the mortgage rate for the duration of the lock period. Until this happens, you don't have a specific rate, it's floating. When a rate is floating, it travels up and down with the market. If the rate was at one level when you initially spoke to a loan officer, and it's since changed by a half percentage point or more, you may be in for a shock. Experienced loan officers will typically provide an interest rate range to account for market fluctuations.

It's always best practice to qualify at the higher end of that range to account for worst-case scenario if the market takes a sudden uptick. Lastly, pay close attention to the lock expiration date. If the loan will not fund until after the expiration date, you will have to extend the lock and there will likely be a fee associated with this.

I must acknowledge there are unscrupulous loan officers that use the old bait and switch approach. This happens when a person is lured into make an application with a promise of an incredibly low interest rate, but it doesn't last.

Soon after committing to work with the loan officer things change. When borrowers consider the pressure from an imminent closing date combined with the unsavory option of starting from scratch with someone else, most soldier on and close the loan. This is unfortunate and completely avoidable if you disregard internet rates from the start no matter how tempting they appear. Choosing a lender based on an advertised internet rate can be like buying spoiled meat just because it's on sale. It may look like a great deal but in the end, you'll regret it. Instead, choose a loan officer that is competent, knowledgeable and easy to work with. Chances are infinitely better you will get what was promised and have a smooth experience.

CHAPTER 6

5 MOST COMMON MISTAKES BORROWERS MAKE WHEN CHOOSING A LENDER

IT'S BEEN MY EXPERIENCE MOST people would rather have a root canal than apply for a mortgage. Hey, when you get a root canal at least they give you anesthesia! OK, I'm being a bit melodramatic, but the reticence many have when applying for a mortgage is real. It's often based on fear of the unknown and horror stories they've read, heard from others, or experienced first-hand. I've heard some of these stories, and my heart breaks for the people that have endured them. Here are the top five mistakes and how you can avoid them.

1) **Selecting a lender by the lowest interest rate only.** If we asked a group of borrowers to identify the most important part of a mortgage, the response would be swift and nearly unanimous, the interest rate. The truth however, is that barometer is entirely wrong. Shocking? Yes. Any less true? Not one iota. I'll prove it.

I'd like you to think of your shoe size. What is it? Don't worry no one else will know. Consider your favorite shoe brand and color. Can you see it? Now imagine finding that shoe on an unbelievable sale. Your favorite shoe, color, and brand at a fraction of the cost. As you reach for the last pair, you can't believe your fortune until you discover it's three sizes too small. What do you do? Do you purchase it anyway and tough it out since it's a great deal? Of course not.

Well, that's exactly what happens when you shop for a mortgage by the rate. Is it the right product for your needs? How does the loan fit into your overall financial picture? Qualifying for the lowest interest rate is simple, have a credit score above 780, put down at least 30%, get no more than a 15-year term, and have a debt to income ratio below 30%. The question is however, is doing this the right move for your family? Does it make sense to put $60,000.00 or more into the walls of your home and maintain unsecured debt? Is your emergency fund at the recommended level? Is your retirement adequately funded? You get the point. Your mortgage has a tremendous impact on your financial picture and must be evaluated accordingly. What's most important is finding the right fit for your specific situation. That may or may not be the mortgage with the lowest rate.

2) **Having your credit pulled after you've applied for a mortgage.** Don't let anyone, and I mean anyone, pull your credit once you've applied for a loan. The best time to compare lenders is before you have your credit pulled, not after. Once your credit is pulled, it's necessary for you to preserve your scores. Additional inquiries can have a negative impact on your scores, and there is no scenario where lowering your scores is good for you. Lower scores can mean an increase in rate or not being able to qualify altogether. Don't risk it!

3) **Working with an order filler.** We've all visited our favorite restaurant, stomach grumbling, and placed an order for our favorite meal. There's nothing like it. While this experience can be rewarding at a fine dining establishment, you don't want the same treatment from your loan officer.

If you are like most people, you will go through the mortgage process five times or less in your life. Those experiences are typically spaced out with several year gaps and things change, a lot. Can you imagine doing your job based only on the experience you had from seven or eight years ago?

That wouldn't work, would it? I'd imagine things change rapidly in your profession on a consistent basis. The mortgage business is the same way. Programs come and go. Products are available today that weren't a year ago; the reverse is also true. Your mortgage professional should be up to date on the latest programs and options available to you.

If you insist on telling them exactly what you want beware, you may get it, even if it isn't the best option for you. It's far better to share your goals and expectations for your home and mortgage and be open to suggestions on how best to accomplish them. If your loan officer doesn't provide options or seems puzzled by your request, find a new one. Your lender should use their expertise and experience to help you choose the best product for your family. You will make the ultimate decision so don't be shy about asking for alternatives and benefit from your lender's input.

4) **Working with someone you will never meet.** In this age of convenience and technological advances, some things are still done best in person. Most professional positions require several interview types before choosing the right candidate.

The process begins with electronic resume filtering, HR reviews, phone screens and in-person interviews to cap off the process. Employers understand the importance of seeing how a candidate responds in person to various questions. How well do they mesh with the team? Do they possess the expertise and soft skills to bring value to the organization? Companies could hire without ever meeting candidates, but most don't because the in-person interaction is invaluable.

Selecting a loan officer to take care of your largest investment requires the same level of dedication. Five minutes of face to face interaction will tell you more than several phone and email conversations ever will. Are they organized, credible, rude, hurried, or attentive? Do they make you feel comfortable or were they aloof and condescending? Expertise is a must, but it must be paired with a personality and philosophy that makes you want to do business with them. An in-person meeting will pay big dividends towards locating that right person. If the lender doesn't measure up after your initial meeting, find another one. You have options. When you find the right one for your family, it will be apparent and worth it.

Getting prequalified instead of preapproved. We have all heard those enticing advertisements that shout an incredible offer with raised voice only to weaken or remove it altogether with an auctioneer like disclaimer at the end. This misleading practice sets false expectations and is nothing more than an overt attempt to get you into the dealership or destination for you to get the rest of the details. A prequalification offer is very much like that. It does not require a full income or credit review; it's essentially a best guess based on what we hope the documentation supports.

Obtaining a mortgage requires meticulous attention to detail. Failing to properly validate income or review all factors can lead to improper expectations and disappointment. Insist on a preapproval. A preapproval requires a thorough credit review, validation of income and assets and an automated underwriting decision. Taking this step has several benefits: it provides a greater peace of mind since the likelihood of final approval is much higher, it gives you much more leverage when submitting an offer to purchase and allows things to move faster when the process begins. Do yourself a favor and insist on a preapproval letter before shopping for your home. You will be happy you did.

CHAPTER 7

HOW MUCH MONEY WILL YOU NEED AT CLOSING?

IF YOU WANT TO MAKE a cake, you'll need several ingredients to make it successfully. Figuring out how much money you need at closing is very similar. The ingredients/components are down payment, closing costs and credits. We'll explore each of these options individually to give you a clear understanding of what to expect.

A down payment is the difference between the loan amount and purchase price and represents your willingness to share in the risk with your lender. Let's say you are purchasing a $300,000.00 home and get a loan for $285,000.00. The difference of $15,000.00 would represent a 5% down payment. Some programs don't require a down payment at all and will provide 100% financing, or a $300,000.00 loan in this example. To obtain better terms however, you will need a down payment of some amount.

The next component to consider is closing costs. These costs are broken into three areas: origination, third party costs and prepaids. Origination costs are fees your lender charges to do the loan. Discount points are also considered part of origination costs. (A discount point is a percentage of the loan, paid at closing to the lender in exchange for a lower rate. Not every loan includes discount points, but they are included in the origination calculation when present.) Origination charges may have different names like application fees, commitment fees, etc. No one works for free. You are going to pay something directly or indirectly in the form of a higher rate to get the mortgage. Make sure you know what these costs are right up front.

Third party costs are fees paid to parties other than the lender that aren't prepaids. This includes the appraiser, attorney or settlement agent, title insurance, credit report, home and pest inspectors; the list could go on. Many people have a part in a successful mortgage closing which is one of the many reasons real estate is so essential to our economy. A mortgage typically represents the largest investment you will ever make. It's not cheap, it's just worth it!

Prepaids are exactly what the name suggests; items paid in advance. This includes mortgage interest, hazard insurance, taxes, and mortgage insurance. Prepaids are usually charges for items you pay on a reoccurring monthly basis, but some portion is required upfront to complete the loan.

The last area that impacts the amount of money you will need to close are credits. Credits can come from the lender, seller, realtor or builder and includes monies you've paid prior to closing. (i.e. earnest monies, due diligence, appraisal costs.) Most homes sell with some sort of incentive from the seller or builder and can greatly reduce the out of pocket amount from closing costs. It's important to note that lending programs have varying amounts that are acceptable as credits. Your lender will confirm the maximum allowable amounts for your specific program.

Now that we've discussed these areas use the following formula to determine your out-of-pocket costs:

Down Payment (DP) + Closing Costs (CC) - Credits (CR) = Cash to Close (CTC)

Let's assume you are purchasing a $300,00.00 home with:
DP = $15,000.00 (5%)
(+)
CC=$8,000.00 (1% origination $3,000.00, third party costs $3,000.00, prepaids $2,000.00)
(-)

CR= $11,000.00 ($6,000.00 seller paid costs, $2,000.00 earnest money, $2,000.00 due diligence deposit, $1,000.00 appraisal and pest inspection**)

$15,000.00 + $8,000.00 = $23,000.00 – $11,000.00 = $12,000.00 CTC

** Although your out-of-pocket costs prior to closing impact the amount needed to close, it is a different figure. Make sure you understand the items you'll need to pay before getting to the closing table. This area is often overlooked by first time homebuyers.

CHAPTER 8

THE SILENT EARTHQUAKE

HAVE YOU EVER EXPERIENCED AN EARTHQUAKE? I've seen unsettling images of enormous buildings twisting as if auditioning for Dancing with the Stars. Shelves are unceremoniously emptied, and streets crack open like cage free eggs for breakfast. If that weren't enough, aftershocks can occur for days without notice. Like shadows, they extend far past the event as reminders of the danger that lurks beneath us. What can be more terrifying?

As frightening as a physical earthquake can be, we've experienced a silent quake with much greater repercussions. With little fanfare or notice, the event has long passed but the tsunami is beginning to crest the horizon. The invisible cause of which I speak, is the transition of responsibility of the American worker to provide for their own retirement.

As the world shrunk, and the implications of a global marketplace were felt, the necessity of removing a titanic-sized drag to a company's bottom line was apparent. Pensions were incredible promises from long ago where loyalty and service to a company were rewarded with a consistent livable benefit for the rest of an employee's natural life. The best and brightest were engaged to leverage their extraordinary skills to make good on the promise of financial security for employees and their families. This agreement however, was retracted with more skill than a street hustler playing three card monte. Like a car without brakes barreling down a winding road with steep cliffs, we must give our complete attention to this dilemma or face the inevitable consequences. Am I exaggerating? I'll let you decide.

Identifying a universal formula for the amount of money needed at retirement can be complicated. We will use the conservative view that a family should accumulate 10 times their household income to retire. Household income recently crested to $57,617.00.[1]

The average lifespan for Americans is 78.8 years.[2] Although many will blow by that age like a race car on the track and live to 90 and beyond.

Using these numbers will give us to a little more than $576,000.00 as a nest egg target by age 65 for retirement. How are retirees doing so far? The average amount retirees have saved at retirement age is $163,577.00.[3] That's a shortfall of $412,423.00, barely 28% of what is needed!

As startling as those numbers are, roughly 1 in 3 families have $5,000.00 or less at retirement. Can you feel the aftershock?

References:

1) https://www.census.gov/library/publications/2017/acs/acsbr16-02.html

2) https://www.cdc.gov/nchs/fastats/life-expectancy.html

3) https://www.cnbc.com/2017/04/07/how-much-the-average-family-has-saved-for-retirement-at-every-age.html

CHAPTER 9

CONVENTIONAL MORTGAGE ADVICE

"**IDEALLY YOU SHOULD SAVE UP** 20% of the home's purchase price to use as your down payment. It's a big number but putting down this much in cash means you only finance 80% of the purchase. That means, you won't have to deal with private mortgage insurance (PMI) and your monthly payments will be much more affordable.

Coming to the table with more cash also makes you a more appealing borrower for lenders. You'll likely secure a better interest rate if you reach the 20% down payment threshold." *Clark Howard*[1]

"You're still in that $225,000.00 home 10 years later. The 15-year mortgage has been paid down to about $98,000.00. However, the balance on a 30-year mortgage is only down to $188,000.00. What does this mean exactly?

It means that if you have a 30-year mortgage, you've paid almost $162,000.00, but you've only knocked

$36,000.00 off the loan. So, over the past 10 years, you've given the bank $130,000.00! Wouldn't it be worth it to pay a little extra every month, so you could avoid that?" *Dave Ramsey*[2]

What do you do when you want to learn more about a topic? If you are like most people, your favorite search engine is fired up and called into action. However, sifting through the avalanche of results can be intimidating. The essence of conventional mortgage advice is captured in four statements; get the lowest rate, take the shortest possible term, pay off the loan as quickly as possible and make as large a down payment as you can afford. Now just wait a minute, you may say. What's wrong with that advice? Nothing, and everything!

If you've ever had the opportunity of cooking or coordinating food for a large group, you know there are a multitude of considerations. Dietary restrictions, allergies and meal preferences are just few things to ponder. It would be unthinkable to try to serve everyone the same thing just because that meal was recommended by a friend. What if the food contains nuts and a guest is severely allergic? Will that succulent filet mignon be enjoyed by a vegetarian? I could go on, but you catch my drift.

If something as simple as a meal requires this level of individual consideration, how much more is warranted for the largest investment most of us will ever make? There are instances where conventional mortgage advice is appropriate and could be applied; it really depends on the situation. The challenge I see for many homeowners, is this advice is universally prescribed and followed without consideration of its appropriateness. Let's consider a summary of each of the conventional mortgage advice pillars.

Get the Lowest Rate

A mortgage interest rate is the rate of return a lender requires to embrace the risk of lending their money. The Bankers Secret was a popular book that extolled the virtues of paying off a mortgage as soon as possible to reduce the amount of interest a mortgage lender received. It showed in startling clarity the power of compounding interest and how its application to a mortgage can require a repayment of significantly more than the original loan amount. It stands to reason then, that one of the best ways to reduce the amount due is to obtain a loan at the lowest possible interest rate.

Get the Shortest Term

The amount of interest ultimately paid is determined by the rate of return, or interest rate, and duration of time interest is compounded.

Mortgage terms can vary from 10 to 40 years. The longer the term, the more time interest compounds and accumulates. Conventional advice recommends obtaining the shortest possible term to reduce the amount of interest payments.

Pay Off the Loan as Quickly as Possible

When I was a child, I remember using the now antiquated concept of layaway. If you are scratching your head as to the meaning of this mysterious concept, I'll explain. Layaway was a method of reserving an item, or items, by making payments on a predetermined scheduled until you made the final payment and completed the purchase. If anticipation got the better of you, you could even make extra, unscheduled payments to hasten the date when you would get your treasures. I still remember fondly the excitement of making that final payment and watching with wide-eyed wonder as my wares were delivered. Conventional mortgage wisdom applies the same principle and recommends extra principal payments whenever possible. That includes bi-weekly payments, annual payments and small amounts of extra principal payments as often as you can.

Make as Large A Down Payment as You Can

A mortgage down payment is simply the difference between the loan amount and sales price.

If you are purchasing a home for $300,000.00 and get a loan for $285,000.00, the difference of $15,000.00 would represent the down payment amount. If you put down less than 20% of the purchase price, or $60,000.00 in this example, you will typically have to pay for mortgage insurance. (Mortgage insurance helps insulate the lender from a loss because of foreclosure.) Premiums for this coverage can vary widely and may be substantial. Conventional advice recommends making at least a 20% down payment to avoid mortgage insurance and lower your monthly mortgage payment.

References:

1) *http://clark.com/homes-real-estate/4-ways-get-best-deal-mortgage/*

2) *https://www.daveramsey.com/blog/the-truth-about-mortgages*

CHAPTER 10

IS IT ALWAYS BEST TO GO WITH THE LOWEST RATE?

TO QUALIFY FOR THE LOWEST RATE simply make a down payment of at least 30% have a credit score above 780, a debt to income ratio below 30% and a loan term of no more than 15 years. Let's assume you can qualify for that, does it always make sense to take the loan with the lowest rate?

Let's change gears for a moment and completely put mortgages aside. Instead of considering a loan let's pretend you are investing money. I have a beauty for you, it offers a whopping 0% rate of return. You read that right, 0%. The investment is not liquid. You may gain access to a portion of your initial investment if you meet my qualifying criteria only. If you do, you can borrow a portion, but you will have to pay me interest for that privilege. If you don't meet my criteria you do not have access to your money at all. Like any investment, it's not guaranteed.

You may gain money, lose a portion or all of it. Lastly don't be alarmed this investment has been around for quite some time and a lot of people are doing it.

How much money would you give me for this investment? I can imagine you trying to jump through the pages to strangle me right now! The truth is, if you are making a large mortgage down payment you are already investing in it. This investment is equity you pay for.

If you have credit card and other debt is it best to use $50,000.00 or more as a down payment? I'll share a real example with you. I had a person reach out to me to get information about a refinance. He ran a cleaning business and purchased a home for $150,000.00. He followed the conventional advice and made a down payment of $50,000.00 to avoid paying mortgage insurance and have a lower monthly payment. Unfortunately, as is the case with many business owners, cashflow ebbed a bit more than it flowed, and he missed a couple of payments. He was able to get back on track and thought he would borrow some of his initial down payment that was now equity in his home. He wanted to have a little more of a nest egg to weather the lean times. I'm sure you can guess what happened when he went to his bank to ask for this money. They passed him an application, ran his credit and denied the loan. He did not qualify to get any of his initial down payment! Can you imagine that?

He options were to hope things didn't continue to slide and manage it the best way he could or sell the home loved. No one should be in this situation but far too many are. They've learned the hard way that getting the lowest rate is not always the best option.

CHAPTER 11

2 TYPES OF EQUITY

Equity You Pay For

Equity can be defined as the difference between the value of an asset and its corresponding liability. Simply put, it is the difference between what you own and owe.

The first kind of equity in a house is the type you pay for. John and Becky purchased a $150,000.00 house and put down $50,000.00 as a down payment. They have a $100,000.00 mortgage with a 30-year term at 5% with a fully amortizing payment. * The Principal & Interest (P&I) portion of this monthly mortgage payment is $536.82.

(A fully amortizing mortgage payment is a payment with both principal and interest allocations. Every time a payment is made a portion of that payment reduces the outstanding principal balance and pays the interest or the cost of using the money for that month.)

John and Becky would have an instant equity position of 33% resulting from their down payment of $50,000.00. ($150,000.00 Purchase Price - $50,000.00 Down Payment = $100,000.00 Loan Balance) Equity would increase each month by the principal amount of their mortgage payment. In this example, at the end of twelve months they would have approximately $1,500.00 in additional equity from monthly mortgage payments. If they make extra principal payments, equity would increase by the amount of those principal payments as well.

Equity from Market Appreciation

The second type of real estate equity occurs because of market appreciation. When we purchase a home, we expect its value to increase over time. The amount it increases can vary widely depending on the home type and its location, but the expectation is that it appreciates over time.

In our example, John and Becky's original home's value was $150,000.00. Let's assume it grows at 2% a year. In 10 years, their home would be worth a little more than $183,000.00. The equity from market appreciation would be $33,000.00. (The difference between the $150,000.00 original value and the estimated value in 10 years of $183,000.00.)

In 10 years, they decide it's time to move and sell the home. They have:

- Approximately $18,600.00 in equity from normal monthly mortgage payments + $50,000.00 from the initial down payment = $68, 600.00 of equity they've paid for.
- $33,000.00 in equity resulting from the homes market appreciation.
- John and Becky have $101,600.00 in total equity.

When the home is sold their profit comes from the difference between what they owe on the home and what it's worth.

Over 30% of their total equity came from market appreciation! This kind of equity happens irrespective of the type and size of the mortgage. In fact, it's not tied to the mortgage whatsoever.

How a Home's Value is Determined

Real estate appraisals are not directly based on tax value, listing price or lucky numbers. The fair market value is based on what similar homes sold for, adjusted for differences, at a specific time in a determined area. For example, if three homes sold in the last several months in John and Becky's neighborhood that are similar in square footage, design and age to theirs, they may be good comparables to use in determining the fair market value of their home.

Their home would receive adjustments in the form of additions or subtractions in appraised value based on its features compared to the other homes. If the other three homes sold for $200,000.00 $197,000.00 and $195,000.00 respectively our estimate of a $183,000.00 value for their home may be little low. This is an intentional oversimplification of the appraisal process, but it's sufficient to illustrate how a home's value is established. Sites like Zillow and Realtor.com may be helpful in providing estimates, but an appraisal is the only way to get a true valuation of a property. It's important to note that home appraisals are part science and art. If several appraisers reviewed the same property they may appraise it at different valuations. The lender ultimately determines whether a value is acceptable and always reviews appraisals thoroughly.

Why is it important for you understand this? I'll elaborate. When we experienced the housing bust in the late 2000's, homes values were reduced by half or more in many places. Homes that had not changed in look, function or features were suddenly worth less because other homes that were comparable to them sold at much lower values.

If we change our example and assume the home sales in John and Becky's neighborhood were $130,000.00 $125,000.00, and $110,000.00.

With these comparable values, is it likely they can sell their home at $183,000.00 if several similar homes sold for much less? Not at all. We'll come back to these implications in just a moment. Now that you understand the two sources of real estate equity, let's explore the characteristics of this unbelievable investment introduced in the previous chapter.

0% Rate of Return

John and Becky made an initial down payment of $50,000.00 to avoid mortgage insurance, reduce the monthly payment and qualify at a better rate. Did they have to use real money to make that down payment? Absolutely. When they made this investment, how much money did the bank give them for the use of their money over the next ten years? What do you mean, you may ask? The bank doesn't ever pay anyone when they get a down payment for a mortgage, they didn't make anything. Interesting!

How about when John and Becky make normal principal or extra principal payments? How much do they earn on those? Nada again. Hmmm, that's fascinating! Am I suggesting that when a bank gets a down payment and any sort of principal payments, scheduled or otherwise, they don't pay one red penny for that money? Yes, that's exactly right!

What do you think the bank* does with that money? Do they lend it out? You betcha! Do you think they receive a 0% rate of return when they lend John and Becky's money? Not a chance. They get free money that reduces their risk in John and Becky's home and use those monies to earn a profit. What a sweet deal! I can see why banks love this investment, but how sound is it for John and Becky?

It's Not Liquid

John and Becky invested $50,000.00 in their mortgage down payment. Their real hard-earned money was used to make that investment. We've also established they are not receiving any return from the bank that is using their monies to earn a profit. Unfortunately, John and Becky's daughter Lisa had an unexpected major medical emergency and will require serious surgery after they've lived in their home for two years.

Although they've established an emergency fund and have health insurance, the out-of-pocket costs are more than they can handle at one time. What should they do? Liquidate their emergency fund and use credit cards for the difference? Take a loan from their retirement account or somewhere else? After much deliberation they come up with a much better idea.

 * Banks used for illustrative purposes. Mortgage investors come in many forms, but the concept remains the same.

They go back to the bank where they make a $50,000.00 down payment to get some of their money back. John and Becky, explain their dire circumstances and ask for a portion of their down payment. They are pointed to the loan officer and given a mortgage application.

Rates have risen considerably since they initially purchased the home. The loan officer gives them three options: 1) Sell their home. 2) Apply for a new mortgage with a cash out designation. 3) Apply for an equity line.

None of these options are good, they love their home. Lisa has lifelong friendships with other kids in the neighborhood. The community is amazing, and the schools are excellent. This is where they want to live for the next several years, moving is not an option. That leaves loans as the alternative and they must qualify to get them. Another family learns the hard truth that their investment is not liquid, and the ramifications are serious.

You Must Qualify to Access It

John and Becky are staring at a mortgage application, disheartened.

They provided their money to the bank, have never been paid for it and now in their time of need must jump through hoops to qualify to get a portion of their own money back. Fortunately, they can qualify for a loan but are not excited about paying to access their own money. Either alternative will signal a major shift in their financial outlook and can potentially derail their plans.

As bleak as this picture may seem, imagine if they were not able to qualify for a new loan? That would mean the only way they could access their money is to sell their home quickly and hope they can recoup their initial investment with some appreciation. Often, that's not an option.

It's Not Guaranteed

Things are not promising for John and Becky. They were shocked to learn that quite a few homes like theirs, sold for less than what they purchased their home for initially. Recently, several large employers in the area had massive layoffs, and many families have sold their homes to move to other places and start over. They can only sell their home for $140,000.00 and will have to pay realtor fees from that amount. Instead of making money they've lost $10,000.00 of their initial investment.

That represents a 20% loss in real money, ouch! They've learned too late that a home's value is not guaranteed.

Everybody Does It

Like John and Becky, people have been making this sort of investment for as long as mortgages have existed. Today, we have choices about the amount of money we allocate to this investment and cannot afford to make the same decisions our grandparents made in vastly different circumstances. Remember when your mother said, "if everybody jumps off a bridge, would you?". Yep, it applies to this situation too.

I've used this realistic situation, to illustrate one of the weaknesses in the conventional mortgage philosophy. Preparing for the worst, and hoping for the best, is a sound financial approach. Unfortunately, job loss, illness and unexpected life changes are the order of the day. Statistically, it's not a matter of if, but when they will occur.

Best-case scenario, if none of these happen in the ten years John and Becky own their home, can they really afford to sideline $50,000.00? Conventional mortgage advice encourages implementing this philosophy, and many use the same approach of a large down payment and extra principal payments with future home purchases further complicating this fragile situation.

The Extraordinary Power of Compound Interest

Which would you rather have, a penny a day that doubles or $10,000.00 a day for 30 days?

If you take the penny a day that doubles, you only earn one cent on the first day. You receive two cents on day two. Day three's take is a whopping four cents. By day seven your up to sixty- four cents bringing your weekly total to $1.27.

On the other side of the proposal if you accepted the $10,000.00 a day you will have accumulated $70,000.00 by the end of the first week.

Day eight, on the penny a day plan finds you raking in $1.28. Day nine yields $2.56 Your cumulative two- week total is $81.92. With the $10,000.00 a day plan you have added another $70,000.00 to your earnings bringing your 14-day total to $140,000.00. If you chose the penny plan, have you started to regret it?

The third week brings more growth, but at its conclusion, we're 70% complete and the gulf between the two options seems insurmountable. The penny a day total has grown to just shy of $22,000.00 but there are only nine days left. The $10,000.00 a day account stands at $210,000.00.

The phenomenal power of compounding interest explodes in the last nine days to find you earning over 5.3 million dollars on day 30 alone with the penny a day plan. The total monthly earnings with this option skyrocket to over 10 million dollars compared to the paltry sum of $300,000.00 from the $10,000.00 a day alternative. No wonder Albert Einstein referred to compound interest as the eighth wonder of the world!

Two lessons leap off the page from this illustration: Get money working for you as soon as possible no matter how small the amount. Nothing can replace time. The more you have, the greater opportunity for explosive growth.

What would have happened if the last nine days of this example were removed? The penny plan would never have come close to the $10,000.00 a day option. Understanding and applying this this concept is a vital part of how Warren Buffet and countless others have built enormous wealth. It's also foundational to understanding a weakness with conventional mortgage advice. Investing large sums of money at 0% for decades can have catastrophic implications for your family's stability and independence.

Investopedia.com defines the Time Value of Money as the idea that money available now is worth more than the same amount in the future due to its potential earning capacity. Check out this powerful Cost of Waiting Calculator from Ativa.com to see this exponential difference this concept makes.

*http://ativa.com/cost-of-waiting-to-***invest-calculator/**

CHAPTER 12

WHAT IS NETWORTH LENDING?

NETWORTH LENDING TEACHES PEOPLE HOW to use their mortgage as a powerful tool to get out of debt sooner and retire with more money. It's a simple concept, but like anything worthwhile, it may take a little effort to fully understand. There are three keystones to this philosophy captured by the acronym **MEA -** *Maximize, Eliminate, Accumulate.*

Maximize

I've heard an anecdote about how psychiatrists would determine if a patient that suffered a bout with insanity had reached the point of recovery. Reportedly, they would put a patient in a room with an overflowing bathtub spilling water onto the floor. The patient would be given a mop and bucket with instructions to clean up the mess.

If they immediately began mopping up the water, it was an indication they were not ready. However, if they turned off the water and then began mopping, it was a sign their reasoning faculties were intact. I have no clue whether that story is factual, but it does illustrate the importance of resolving the source of an issue before trying to move forward. In the same way, the Maximize phase of *NetWorth Lending* is where you assess your current financial picture and economize your efforts to reduce waste. It requires a clear-eyed audit of where you are today, coupled with accurate measurements of your trajectory towards your goals.

<u>Goals</u>

1. How much do you earn per month? (Gross Household Income & Take Home)

2. What is your current monthly mortgage payment or estimated payment if you are a potential homebuyer?

3. What are your mortgage terms? (Interest rate and term.)

4. What are your annual taxes?

5. How much is your mortgage insurance?

6. How much is your homeowner's insurance?

7. How much are the homeowner's association dues?

8. How much did you use or have for a down payment?

9. How much in extra principal payments do you make each month?

10. What is your home's estimated value and purchase price?

11. What is the balance of your current mortgage(s)?

12. How long do you plan to own this home?

13. What are your total monthly living expenses? (Utilities, Food, etc.)

14. How much are the payments for other debts? (Credit cards, installment loans, etc.)
    List each:
    a. Creditor Name
    b. Balance
    c. Interest Rate
    d. Payment Amount
    e. Projected Payoff Date/Remaining Payments

15. When do you want to be debt free? Month and year. (Exclude the mortgage.)

16. How much are you saving each month?

17. How much money do you need for an emergency fund? (If unsure your 6 months of your gross household income.)

18. How much have you saved toward your emergency fund goal?

19. If you continue with your current trajectory, when will you reach your emergency fund goal? Month and year.

20. What age do you want to retire?

21. How much money will you need to retire by this age? (If you are not sure use 10x's your annual household income.)

22. How much have you saved towards this retirement goal?

23. If you continue with your current trajectory, when will you meet your retirement goal? (Month, year and age)

Once you have collected this information, we can identify areas where maximizing should take place. You have clearly identified your goals, and current progress so we can determine if *NetWorth Lending* can improve your situation.

Eliminate

Earlier, I referenced a partial quote from Albert Einstein calling compound interest the eighth wonder of the world. The rest of that quote says" He that understands it, earns it. He that doesn't, pays it." Albert was a smart fellow and the Eliminate phase takes this concept to heart. It's vital to get compound interest working for you while eliminating instances where it's working against you. Once we've identified the places it is, we will create an elimination plan to pay-off debt sooner, excluding the mortgage.

Wait a minute, isn't that double talk? A mortgage is typically the largest debt and has compounding interest why wouldn't we attack this also? That's a great question, so glad you asked. There are four reasons. There is a tax benefit to mortgage payments; a mortgage allows you to control an appreciating asset, prepaying your mortgage is not the best use of your money, and you can never get rid of your house payment entirely.

Tax Benefit - We've all heard the quip there are two certainties in life, death and taxes. Tax liability is a big deal and deserves a big part of any wealth building plan. Mortgage interest can be tax deductible and that simple but powerful truth makes mortgages slightly different than other debts. Mortgage interest rates are usually far less than unsecured debt rates. Couple this with the potential tax advantages from mortgage interest payments and individual consideration is warranted. Consult your tax professional to learn more about how this applies to your specific situation.

It Allows You to Control an Appreciating Asset – When we purchase real estate, we expect it to increase in value over time. I don't think anyone would be interested in buying a home they knew would become less valuable than what they bought it for. This expectation is generally supported by history with brief correction periods. A mortgage gives you the ability to control an appreciating asset that even when growing at a small rate can mean a major increase in value. Let's assume you own a $300,000.00 house and it grows at 3% per year. That would mean you would add $9,000.00 in equity to your home in the first year. If you owned that home for 10 years and that appreciation rate remained constant, the home would appreciate by $104,806.00!

If you made a 5% down payment to purchase the home, that $15,000.00 allowed you to control an asset that brought a tremendous return. Credit cards, installment loans or a new car purchase won't do this. Mortgages are in a class of their own.

Prepaying Your Mortgage Is Not the Best Use of Your Money - We've covered this extensively in the Unbelievable Investment section, so I won't reiterate it here. Please re-read that section for a refresher.

You Can Never Entirely Get Rid of Your House Payment. - A house payment is comprised of four parts; Principal and Interest, Taxes, Insurances and Homeowners Association dues. Paying off a mortgage completely will only allow you to reduce your total house payment. You can never eliminate it completely.

Will there ever be a time when you won't need homeowner's insurance? Will you ever reach a point where you will don't have to pay taxes? How about homeowner's association dues? Many rush to eliminate the mortgage portion of their payment without considering they will always have the other portions as long as they own their home. We'll explore the importance of this fact more in the Accumulation phase.

Now that we've established the reason for a mortgage's uniqueness, let's get back to Elimination. You should have the debt payoff date for each of your bills. Next, create a debt rolldown and apply the intel we've obtained from the Maximize phase to the strategically eliminate debts and accelerate your debt freedom date by using the same money more effectively.

The order debts are paid is based on your goals. Is it better to leave student loans and add more income to accumulation efforts? The order and priority are so individually driven that I hesitate to set any more guidelines than I have. Think through each decision and make sure each action takes you closer to your goals of debt freedom and retirement.

ACCUMULATION

What do ants, squirrels and bears all have in common? An uncanny ability to prepare for upcoming changes. Through instinct, they are keenly aware of the importance advance preparation plays in their survival. Retirement is like that in many ways. We are living longer, and skyrocketing healthcare costs consume larger chunks of our budgets. What were supposed to be golden years, have become anything but for too many. The last phase of *NetWorth Lending* focuses on Accumulation. Accumulation is essential! It puts the power of compound interest to work for you, and that can forever tilt the scales of financial independence in your favor.

You Can Never Entirely Get Rid of Your House Payment Part 2 - Why do you really want to pay off your mortgage? I've found most people want to, because it represents their largest monthly expense. Eliminating it, they've reasoned, will put them in a better financial position and help them take a major step toward financial independence.

While I commend and understand that motive, extinguishing the mortgage is not the safest or best path to accomplish that end. Don't misunderstand me, paying off your mortgage can be quite an achievement. It takes extraordinary discipline and commitment to complete. In the end sadly, it's simply not enough to guarantee financial security because you can never completely get rid of your house payment.

Many seniors have experienced the searing pain of losing mortgage free homes. Homes they've raised families and found community in. My city, like many others, is experiencing a revitalization in the downtown and surrounding areas. One of the many changes this type of reinvestment brought is rapidly increasing real estate prices. Homes that were once inexpensively valued have exploded and increased five-fold. Usually increasing home values are desirable, but it can spell doom for owners on fixed incomes. In this situation, taxes and insurance costs grow uncontrollably and demand the lion's share of their income. This sad spiral continues until the owner faces the unbearable choice of selling their home or losing it.

Many in this situation paid off their homes first and accumulated savings second, only to discover they don't have enough to live. What happens then?

Might this explain the recent explosion in reverse mortgages?* When this occurs, unfortunately the only thing passed to the next generation is a big mortgage and hard lesson. If this was what the homeowner really intended, why would they pay off their mortgage only to access their equity in a very costly way? (See link below for more information on reverse mortgages.)

https://www.investopedia.com/terms/r/reversemortgage.asp

The goal must be accumulating enough reserves that the house or any other payment, becomes insignificant. Let's imagine you've accumulated a million dollars. Would a monthly house payment of $2,500.00 make you uneasy? I'll go out on a limb and say probably not, even though that represents $30,000.00 of annual payments. If the taxes and insurance quadrupled, you may not be happy, but could you afford it? Of course! If that's true, isn't the real issue not having enough money saved?

If you really want to pay off your mortgage, be my guest, but why not do it when can afford to write a check for the loan balance and still be financially independent? It doesn't have to be an either-or decision. Both are achievable by simply adjusting the priority of which you pursue first.

When we began talking about *NetWorth Lending*, I said the numbers must always be the determining factor in choosing which option to pursue. Let's compare *NetWorth Lending* to conventional mortgage advice with some examples and see the difference it can make.

2 Families - 3 Scenarios

John and Jane are both 35 years old, have two children and purchased their first home on Elm Street. They love the community, schools and being so close to everything. They've prepared well for their home purchase and made a down payment of 20% to avoid paying mortgage insurance on their $300,000.00 home. They plan to live in this home for at least ten years when their children will graduate from high school. Their household income is $56,000.00 per year. They are saving $300.00 per month towards retirement and making an additional $200.00 a month principal payment to limit the amount of interest they ultimately pay. John and Jane are committed to becoming debt free as soon as possible and are following conventional mortgage advice.

Stan and Dana are 35 years old, have two children and moved next to John and Jane on Elm Street. This was no accident since Stan and John work together, and Dana, Jane and the kids are all great friends.

Stan and Dana also are well prepared for their first home purchase. They opted for the minimum down payment of 3% even though they saved 20% to purchase their $300,000.00 home. They will have to pay mortgage insurance, and plan to move in ten years when their children graduate from high school. They elected to save $500.00 a month and not pay anything to accelerate the mortgage. Stan and Dana want to become debt free as soon as possible and are following the *NetWorth Lending* philosophy.

The third example is for an interest only loan repayment option. It represents the ultimate expression of not investing any money into mortgage principal. With this repayment type, the monthly loan payment is based on interest cost only. Typically, this repayment option is available for some duration of the mortgage term. The following illustration is intended to demonstrate the effectiveness of the concept of *NetWorth Lending* with all major repayment options.

	John & Jane Conventional Advice	Stan & Dana NetWorth Lending	Interest Only NetWorth Lending
House	300,000.00	300,000.00	300,000.00
Rate	4.5	4.625	4.75
Term	360	360	360
DownPayment	60,000.00	9,000.00	9,000.00
Loan Amount	240,000.00	291,000.00	291,000.00
Mortgage Ins	0.00	9,000.00	9,000.00
Monthly Payment	1,216.00	1,496.00	1,188.00
Extra Principal Payments	200.00	0.00	0.00
Retirement	300.00	220.00	528.00
Total Monthly Payments	1,716.00	1,716.00	1,716.00
Savings 5 Years	**22,152.00**	**75,152.00**	**97,894.00**

Taxes, Homeowners Insurance and Homeowners Association dues were omitted for simplicity sake since they would be the same for all.

- *A 7% Rate of return was used for illustrative purposes only and is not investment advice. Please see your financial planner for investment options.*

Murphy's Law

Life is uncertain, and things change fast. A superior mortgage philosophy should work in best and worst- case applications. We will use realistic stress tests to evaluate how each approach performs.

John and Stan received unfortunate news, their office is being downsized. It's been 5 years since they purchased their homes, they are understandably concerned. Immediately after hearing the news John goes to his bank to get a loan against his equity. Unfortunately, with his employment ending soon he is not eligible. Although he has a significant amount of equity, he cannot access it without selling his home.

Stan on the other hand, can focus on his job search. They have sufficient reserves to outlast this scary chapter and keep moving forward. Which family would you rather be? Who is better positioned to handle an unexpected lengthy unemployment? Even if both families decided to sell their home, one can afford to wait for the right price, the other would have to sell for whatever they can get.

In summary, Stan & Dana are better positioned to handle unexpected emergencies without arresting their forward progress. John & Jane are not so fortunate since they are heavily committed to an ineffective investment.

Home Values Drop Drastically

Real estate is one of the surest investments anyone can make. It is an investment, however, and subject to the ups and downs any market can bring. If values plummet and our families' homes are suddenly worth $150,000.00, who is in a better position? Both will lose their initial down payment. Stan & Dana separated as much of their money as possible from their home and are better protected as a result. Both families will have to keep their homes since neither will be able to sell in this depressed market. Only one family will still be able to earn a significant return while they are waiting for the housing market to recover.

Everything Goes According to Plan

If Murphy's law doesn't strike and the things progress seamlessly, let's see how *NetWorth Lending* compares to conventional mortgage advice.

10 Years

We've already explored how things would look at 5 years. At the 10-year mark the impact of the investment choices becomes more apparent.

	John & Jane Conventional Advice	Stan & Dana NetWorth Lending	Interest Only NetWorth Lending
Savings 10 Years	53,221.00	121,649.00	176,289.00

Selling at 10 Years

We determined both families would sell their homes at the ten-year mark. Both purchased a home at the approximate value of their current home as their forever home. John and Jane consistently invested more into the walls of their home and it pays off at this juncture.

They have a lower principal balance and net more money from the sale of their home. Conventional mortgage advice has a slight advantage over the *NetWorth Lending* approach at this period if no major life changes occur that disrupt the initial plan. We'll continue to follow our families' strategies through 30 years and compare the final outcomes.

	John & Jane Conventional Advice	Stan & Dana NetWorth Lending	Interest Only NetWorth Lending
Home Value in 10 Years	404,000.00	404,000.00	404,000.00
Principal Balance	162,175.00	233,985.00	291,000.00
Realtor Fees	24,000.00	24,000.00	24,000.00
Net from Sale	217,825.00	146,015.00	89,000.00
Investment Monies	53,221.00	121,649.00	176,289.00
Total Saving & Sale Proceeds	271,046.00	267,664.00	265,289.00
Difference		-3,382.00	-5,757.00

- *An annual appreciation rate of 3% was used to determine the value of the $300k home in 10 years.*

73

Purchasing a New Home

John and Jane net more from the sale of their home and continue to follow conventional mortgage wisdom. They obtain a 15-year mortgage and make as large a down payment as they can afford. They get a lower interest rate and do not have mortgage insurance. With a smaller mortgage payment, they can begin investing more towards retirement. The investment account of $53,221.00 continues to earn interest for them as well.

Stan and Dana opt for the smallest possible down payment and shoulder the entire cost of mortgage insurance right up front. They are making a small contribution towards their investment account. They chose to get as much money working for them as soon as possible. The interest only option demonstrates the full implementation of not contributing anything towards equity you pay for.

	John & Jane	Stan & Dana	Interest Only
	Conventional Advice	NetWorth Lending	NetWorth Lending
New Home Purchase	400,000.00	400,000.00	400,000.00
Interest Rate	4.5	4.625	4.75
Term	180	360	360
DownPayment	217,825.00	12,000.00	12,000.00
Mortgage Ins	0.00	12,000.00	12,000.00
Loan Amount	182,175.00	388,000.00	388,000.00
Monthly Payment	1,394.00	1,995.00	1,535.83
Extra Principal Payments	0.00	0.00	0.00
Monthly Savings Amount	636.00	35.00	494.00
Total Monthly Payments	2,030.00	2,030.00	2,030.00
Net Proceeds from Sale After New Mortgage	0.00	122,015.00	65,000.00
Investment Monies	53,221.00	121,649.00	176,378.00
Total Net Proceeds & Investment Account	**53,221.00**	**243,664.00**	**242,378.00**
Additional Funds vs Conventional Advice	**0.00**	**190,443.00**	**189,157.00**

- *Taxes, Homeowners Insurance and Homeowners Association dues were omitted for simplicity sake since they would be the same for all.*
- *A 7% Rate of return was used for illustrative purposes only and is not investment advice. Please see your financial planner for investment options.*

	John & Jane	Stan & Dana	Interest Only
	Conventional Advice	NetWorth Lending	NetWorth Lending
Savings 5 Years	121,607.00	344,336.00	376,424.00
Savings 15 Years	352,048.00	683,570.00	828,121.00
Savings 30 years	1,626,305.00	1,932,771.00	2,444,204.00
House Mortgage Balance	0.00	0.00	2,044,204.00
Additional Funds vs Conventional Advice	**0.00**	**306,466.00**	**417,899.00**

- *The full payment of $2030.00 was invested for John and Jane when the mortgage was extinguished.*

- *Taxes, Homeowners Insurance and Homeowners Association dues were omitted for simplicity sake since they would be the same for all.*

- *A 7% Rate of return was used for illustrative purposes only and is not investment advice. Please see your financial planner for investment options.*

Putting it All Together

A young woman is preparing a turkey while her husband looks on. She cuts off the back of the turkey and puts it in the pan. He asks, why did you cut off the end? That's the way you cook a turkey, she retorts. Shocked he protests and they go back and forth until she realizes she only did that because her mother always did.

His question made her curious and she called her mother to ask why she always prepared the turkey this way. Her mother thought for a moment and realized she did because she always saw her mother cook it like that.

They called the matriarch to see if she could solve the mystery. When they asked the question, the wise lady didn't hesitate. She said I always cut off the back of the turkey because my pot was too small!

This story illustrates the importance of doing things with purpose and understanding. Simply continuing an action because that's what some have always done can be dangerous and ineffective.

Do you recall the startling statistic that the average family retires with slightly more than $160,000.00 in investments? This number falls drastically short of the $576,000.00 minimum target and is just a third of our best-case scenario with John and Jane. I intentionally selected the best-case scenario to fairly illustrate the difference in concepts. If everything goes according to plan, conventional mortgage advice leaves John and Jane more vulnerable to life's unexpected changes and eventually costs them hundreds of thousands of dollars in lost income.

What happens if things don't go quite so smoothly? Disaster! Our family's account ends up looking much more like the average than the best-case scenario. Many families encounter hardships while following conventional mortgage wisdom, only to learn too late it isn't enough. I could share painful stories of families that lived through terrible situations but unfortunately, most of us already know someone who has.

I believe *NetWorth Lending* is a viable alternative to help families recapture and maximize their precious resources.

Is it a cure all, the magic bullet? The solution for every situation? No. It is a strategy that can provide your family with more safety and security as you strive for financial independence.

If you grasp the concepts in the book and take the next step to explore how this strategy could work for you, I have accomplished my goal. Ultimately let the numbers be your guide as you determine what the best option is for your family.

If you have questions or would like more information, please contact me at info@networthlending.com

About the Author

NETWORTH LENDING

For more than two decades, Gerald has served in the mortgage industry with distinction. His passion for education and empowerment create client advocates and help him deliver phenomenal results.

Gerald strives to change the transactional way people shop for and obtain mortgages. He believes every person should be treated in a way that reflects their singular importance and helps his clients choose the right mortgage for their unique situation.

www.ingramcontent.com/pod-product-compliance
Lightning Source LLC
Chambersburg PA
CBHW071223220526
45468CB00002B/714

978198357515 0